bettas
in color

by w.l. whitern

completely illustrated with color photograph

TABLE OF CONTENTS

ISBN 0-87666-014-6

Distributed in the U.S.A. by T.F.H. Publications, Inc., 211 West Sylvania Avenue, P.O. Box 27, Neptune City, N.J. 07753; in England by T.F.H. (Gt. Britain) Ltd., 13 Nutley Lane, Reigate, Surrey; in Canada to the book store and library trade by Clarke, Irwin & Company, Clarwin House, 791 St. Clair Avenue West, Toronto 10, Ontario; in Canada to the pet trade by Rolf C. Hagen Ltd., 3225 Sartelon Street, Montreal 382, Quebec; in Southeast Asia by Y.W. Ong, 9 Lorong 36 Geylang, Singapore 14; in Australia and the south Pacific by Pet Imports Pty. Ltd., P.O. Box 149, Brookvale 2100, N.S.W., Australia. Published by T.F.H. Publications, Inc. Ltd., The British Crown Colony of Hong Kong.

This magnificent fish is a male Butterfly Betta, one of a strain developed by Mr. O. Tutwiler of Florida.

GENERAL INTRODUCTION

In the aquarium hobby, popularity is often fleeting. Many are the species of fish that have been imported, enjoyed a short vogue, and then drifted out of the picture, to be seen again only rarely. This is not true of the little Asiatic fish known to aquarists as *Betta splendens*, Siamese Fighting Fish, or just plain Betta. Bettas have been kept and enjoyed by hobbyists almost from the earliest days of the hobby, and there is every indication that they will always retain their favored status.

It is odd that a fish with the temperament of the Siamese Fighting Fish should have achieved such prominence in the hobby. As its common name suggests, *Betta splendens* is no angel. Males of the species will fight with one another almost to the death, and even females can be nasty, especially to their sisters. But although this unhappy trait would seem to put a damper on any hobbyist's enthusiasm for Bettas, it doesn't, because the fish has a characteristic far outweighing the disadvantage presented by its pugnacious nature: it is beautiful.

Our present-day Siamese Fighters owe their beauty to the Orientals who devoted their lives to changing the drab wild Bettas into today's long-finned, multi-hued jewels. This transition was accomplished over the course of a century and is the product of the patience and meticulous attention to detail for which the Asiatic peoples are so well known. And a hard job it was, for our current stocks of Siamese Fighting Fish bear little resemblance to their ancestors. Gone are the fish of murky greenish-brown coloring and stubby, graceless fins; in their place we now have brilliant fish with flowing fins of imperial carriage.

In their native waters in Siam (Thailand), where the Betta's natural animosity towards other males of his species is often put to practical use through the medium of staged fishfights on which considerable sums are wagered, *Betta splendens* lives in rice paddies and other sluggish waters. Many hobbyists might surmise from this that Bettas are able to stand the most deplorable water conditions. Unfortunately, this is not so. Although the fish can do with considerably less space than other species, other conditions must be met, especially in the area of temperature maintenance. This need for higher than average temperatures is particularly important if an attempt at spawning is undertaken. And this is usually the case, because most aquarists who have kept Bettas with any degree of success make a stab at breeding them, for two reasons: raising the fry presents a challenge, and the resulting new crop of fish can be sold for a good price, thus defraying at least part of the hobbyist's expenses.

Now that we've met *Betta splendens* in general, let's go on and study him in more detail.

Two male Bettas, gill plates extended, jockey for position in their fight to dominate one another. Before the actual battle is joined, each will assume different threatening postures. During these activities, the fins will be extended to their fullest, and the colors of the fish will be at their best.

Two other members of the genus **Betta**, **B. bellica** (above) and **B. brederi**. Unlike the Siamese Fighting Fish, **Betta brederi** is a mouthbreeder in which the male (upper fish) carries the eggs in his mouth. Photos: B. bellica by Dr. Herbert R. Axelrod; B. brederi by E. Roloff.

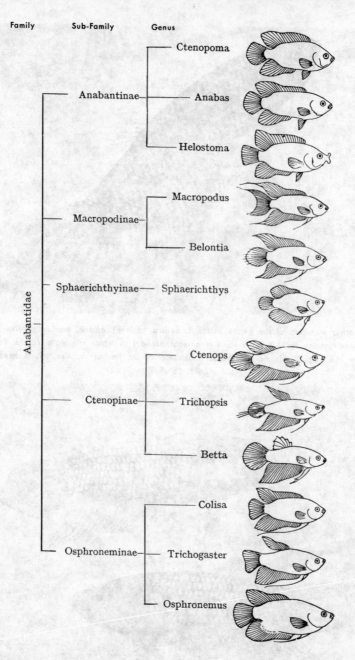

Representatives of the family Anabantidae, all fishes equipped with accessory breathing organs. From the Illustrated Dictionary of Tropical Fishes.

CLASSIFICATION

Siamese Fighting Fish are Anabantids; all fishes within this family can survive in water that has a low concentration of dissolved oxygen, because they are equipped with air-breathing accessory organs which permit air to be taken directly from above the surface of the water. This air is taken in at the mouth and passed to the air-breathing accessory organ known as the "labyrinth".

Because of this air-breathing accessory organ's being designated as a "labyrinth", Anabantids are often referred to as the Labyrinths or Labyrinthine Fishes. Bettas absorb very little dissolved oxygen from the water, being more dependent on the accessory organ than most species within this group.

Many aquarists have a misguided idea that any of the Labyrinths may be introduced into an overcrowded aquarium because they can get their oxygen from the air and will not deplete the supply of dissolved oxygen in the water. This practice is worse than poor: it can even be fatal.

To maintain Bettas in an active and full color state, they must be maintained in water that has a slightly higher temperature than that normally used for other species. A temperature of 78° F. is ideal, but even this should be a few degrees higher for spawning purposes.

At temperatures between 68° and 72° F. Bettas appear to be listless, do not surface as often, and their color pattern and fin-spreading is less conspicuous. These colder temperatures react upon the fish's metabolism to such an extent that a state of semi-dormancy is induced.

Without exception, most Labyrinth Fishes are seen to best advantage if maintained in a fairly large aquarium. Bettas will acclimatize themselves to smaller surroundings, but they look prettier in a big tank.

Although only one male Betta should be maintained in an aquarium, several females may safely be placed together in a community aquarium. Of course, there should be no male present in such an aquarium. Females, although not as strikingly beautiful as the males, do have very interesting color patterns and will enhance any tank. Of all the fishes in the family Anabantidae, Bettas undoubtedly are the most exotic and in the greatest demand by all aquarists.

WATER CONDITIONS

Success in maintaining any fish in captivity is dependent upon several general factors, not the least of which is the provision of correct water conditions. Bettas are no exception to the general rule, and when they appear listless, fail to display fully extended fins, or show less vivid color patterns, it must be assumed that something is wrong. We have already seen that temperature plays an important part in the well-being of the Betta; two other factors, directly related to the chemical composition of the water, play almost equally important roles. These two factors are the hardness of the water and the pH of the water. Water hardness can be defined generally as the amount of dissolved minerals, especially calcium, in any given quantity of water. The pH of water is dependent upon its concentration of hydrogen ions. In short, pH is a measure of water's acid or alkaline properties. On the pH scale, values of less than 7.0 are acid and above 7.0 are alkaline; 7.0 is neutral, neither acid nor alkaline.

There is a great difference between the long-finned male in the upper picture and the short-finned male below; the short-finned male is so far removed from the finnage characteristic of a good male that he could be easily thought to be a female. Both photos by Dr. Eduard Schmidt.

Before attempting to provide the correct water conditions there should be some assessment and appreciation of the water conditions under which wild Bettas live. Bettas are native to waters that have a soft muddy bottom, a condition prevalent in the rice paddies which they inhabit. This indicates that their home waters would be murky and of an amber tinge. It would also be very soft and would not exceed eight degrees of hardness and positively would not have any saline content. It would also be slightly acid but would not be lower than 6.8 pH.

To provide these conditions is not difficult. Soft water (8 DH is considered fairly soft) can be acquired by using demineralized or distilled water in a 50% proportion with normal tap-water or well-water. The acidity and amber tinge can be achieved by suspending a small bag of peat moss in one corner of the aquarium.

There are available at any pet store testing kits for water, both for pH and DH. Each has included full instructions as to its method of operation; they are fairly accurate.

Although Bettas can withstand some minor abuses due to incorrect water conditions, it will definitely affect their general deportment and later may interfere with their breeding potential. Thus the preparation and maintenance of correct water conditions is of prime importance. Healthy, active and colorful fish can be maintained only when correct water conditions are provided.

A male Betta with extensive fin development. Note the contrast between the light body and more deeply colored fins; this is a Cambodia. Photo by Dr. Eduard Schmidt.

FOODS AND FEEDING

Many of the problems that arise, including diseases, can be definitely traced to a lack of understanding in relation to the great importance of supplying correct foods and feeding procedures. It is essential that aquarists should endeavor to acquaint themselves with the foods indigenous to the fishes' native habitat. If there is a preponderance of live animal foods available in these areas, then it is important that every endeavor should be made to duplicate these food conditions. Often this requires that some elements of their food should be supplemented with substitutes.

Bettas are carnivorous and this indicates that animal life and finely scraped raw meats should constitute the majority of their diet. In their native waters, mosquito larvae are in plentiful supply at all times. This same food (alive) is readily available to the hobbyist throughout the summer months, but it must be substituted for during the winter months. Frozen mosquito larvae are available during this period of the year. An excellent substitute can be readily supplied with finely chopped small red garden worms, white worms or newly hatched brine shrimp. The brine shrimp are particularly good. Bettas will accept any of the commercially prepared dry foods, but these normally are not sufficient and must be supplemented with the type of foods already recommended.

When conditioning Bettas for breeding, diet scheduling is very important. As they have very strong teeth, although their alimentary tract is shorter than in other fishes of comparable size, they are equipped to accept finely scraped meats. These should be in the raw state and fed quite frequently.

It is very important for aquarists to experiment for a few days with specific types of foods; careful observation should enable the hobbyist to determine which foods are most suited.

Care must be taken to assure that over-feeding does not take place. Uneaten foods quickly decompose and foul the water to an extent that may be dangerous. Foul water harbors unwanted bacterial colonies which may be the direct or secondary cause of many of the internal fish diseases. Such diseases do not readily respond to medication. Time devoted to preparing proper feeding schedules and diets containing a high nutritive value is well spent. It can be instrumental in avoiding unnecessary problems.

DISEASES AND MEDICANTS

Maintaining fish in a healthy condition should always be of prime consideration. This is far more simple than trying to effect a cure for a diseased fish, because many diseases are neither readily detected nor readily medicated, and there is always the danger that in curing a disease there may be after-effects that have far more serious effects upon the fish than the disease itself.

Healthy fish are quite capable of withstanding many diseases through natural resistance, but when they are in poor health this resistance is lowered. Far too often Bettas suffer from malnutrition induced by improper feeding schedules and poor quality foods.

Many diseases require several days to develop before presenting any visible signs. Aquarists should always make a careful daily observation of their fishes. If any suddenly display unusual behavior, sores, or wounds and darkened areas on the body, these should be immediately isolated into a separate aquarium. Daily observations will detect any further developments. Once the symptoms are sufficiently clear to permit the disease to be diagnosed, immediate treatment and medication should be given.

There are available today many commercially prepared medicants, including the new wonder drugs and antibiotics. The use of these should be approached discreetly because of possible complications later. Undoubtedly many of these medicants will effect a cure but fishes, like people, can build up a resistance to these new wonder drugs and antibiotics. This indicates that with a repetition of any disease the medicant would be non-effective, or at least less effective.

There is also a general belief, not yet fully proven, that many of the wonder drugs and antibiotics have a definite effect upon the reproductive organs. This is indicated by a deterioration of the stock derived from spawnings. In some instances they appear to be much smaller, and they are fewer in number.

It is never advisable to hurry a cure for any disease; many diseases have a specific time cycle, and the application of additional medicants will not hurry the cure. Furthermore, it is dangerous to use larger dosages than those prescribed for any given medicant. Many medicants contain ingredients that are harmless if used as prescribed, but dosages in excess of the prescribed amount may be lethal.

In many instances, either disease or wounds are of such proportions that any attempt to medicate is useless. It is more humane to destroy an infected fish under such conditions.

Never gamble with disease; if it strikes an aquarium and is contagious, remove all fish immediately and place them into isolation, separating those that have visual symptoms of disease into another aquarium. The aquarium from which the diseased fish have been removed should be stripped down. The sand or gravel should be sterilized by pouring boiling hot water over it. The plants should be sterilized by immersion in an alum solution, and any rocks or driftwood should be treated in a similar manner. The aquarium should be thoroughly sterilized with a strong salt solution.

To the more serious aquarist, additional equipment, such as a small microscope, a good magnifying glass and a small set of scales, is invaluable. Many fine specimens can be cured of a disease provided the necessary equipment and medicants are immediately available. Delay will often cause the disease to spread to such proportions that medication fails to be effective. Here are some common Betta ailments and their description and cure.

White Spot (*Ichthyophthirius*). Every aquarist at some time or other has had to face the problem of clearing up an aquarium containing fish having this disease. Generally the accepted theory for the cause is a sudden drop in the water temperature. To some extent this is correct in the majority of infections, but fish in a state of malnutrition will also be readily susceptible to the same disease.

First visual indication of its presence is the appearance of small white spots; these spots usually show first on the fins, later on the body.

Each of these spots indicates that the responsible parasite—*Ichthyophthirius*—has penetrated through the fish's skin into the tissue. Actually, the infection takes place several days prior to the appearance of the white spots, but about five days are usually required for the parasite to go through this first stage.

11

Th finnage of this blue male Betta is not fully extended; under excitement, he would be even more beautiful.

The ventral fins of this male red Betta do not show the white tips which are present on many male specimens. Photo by Dr. Herbert R. Axelrod.

No other fish has inspired artists as much as has the Betta; highly stylized, these drawings show the artists' admiration for their subject.

This is known as the stage of "metamorphosis," in which the parasite passes through a complete change of appearance and condition.

After this period, the new form leaves the body as a hard-cased cyst. Upon leaving its host, the cyst slowly sinks to the bottom of the aquarium, lodging on any obstacle it may come in contact with on the way.

The period of incubation within these cysts is approximately five days, after which they burst open, releasing several hundred more perfectly formed and active young parasites.

There are several recommended medications for effecting a cure: methylene blue, strong common salt solutions, and the many commercially prepared medicants. These latter include some of the new wonder drugs or antibiotics. Undoubtedly they do effect a cure, but caution should be exercized in their use. Very little is known of the actual after-effects, particularly in relation to breeding potential.

From the viewpoint of safety, use quinine hydrochlorate. This is easily available at the drug store in five-grain capsules. Use one capsule for each ten gallons of water in the infected aquarium. If no appreciable change is seen after three days, the same dosage can be repeated without any harmful effects upon the fish.

When all white spots have disappeared from the infected fish, add two drops of 2% Mercurochrome to each gallon of water. This will destroy any of the parasites remaining in the infected aquarium. Allow one day for complete medication, then remove fifty per cent of the water, replacing with fresh tap water. It is very important that not more than two drops per gallon of the Mercurochrome are used, or it may cause distress to the fish. This medicant has toxic properties if used in too large a dose.

Velvet Disease (*Oodinium*). Bettas are very susceptible to this disease, in common with most other Asiatic species.

The first indication of Velvet is the appearance of a yellowish fuzz slightly below the dorsal fin. This spreads rapidly until the whole of the back becomes covered.

There is much controversy as to whether or not an effective cure is possible by direct medication. Many experts advise the use of five pennies to each gallon of water in the infected aquarium. Their theory is that the copper in the pennies sets up a reaction with the acids in the aquarium water. This produces small quantities of dissolved copper salts which are lethal to the parasites responsible for this disease.

Another method is to get two pieces of copper sheeting, around $1\frac{1}{2}$ inches square. Attach an insulated wire to each. Place one piece at each end of the aquarium and attach the wires to a 4-volt dry cell battery. Permit the current to pass through the aquarium water for several hours. There are no recorded instances in relation to the after-effects of this medication or whether or not it effects a permanent cure.

A certain degree of success has been achieved by removing the infected fish to a well saturated soft cloth. Swab the infected areas well with a 2% solution of household ammonia first. Then swab with a 5% solution of Argyrol. Although there is no definite guarantee that this medication does effect a permanent cure, it at least gives temporary relief. It can be assumed that it is a far safer method of medicating than any others recommended. This disease is fairly contagious, so possibly the best method to adopt is to destroy any infected fish as soon as it is noticed to have this disease.

14

The combative tendencies of Siamese Fighting Fish leaves them open to many wounds on the body and around the mouth. Sometimes a wound, if left untreated, will be attacked by the fungus **Saprolegnia**, which is evidenced by a whitish fuzz in the immediate area of the sore. As soon as such symptoms are noted, treatment should be begun. Photo by Dr. Herbert R. Axelrod.

Fungus (*Saprolegnia*). Any fish infected with this disease should be considered to be in a secondary stage of infection. This fungus will show itself on the outer ridges of any wounds that have been acquired through fighting or hitting against a jagged rock. Whenever a fish, particularly a Betta, suffers a wound, the wound should be treated immediately, to prevent fungus.

A sure medication is to put the infected fish into a strong solution of common salt and let it remain until it shows signs of distress. Then remove the fish to a well saturated soft cloth and swab the wounds with 5% Argyrol. Repeat daily until the wound and fungus have completely healed.

Finally, it is always beneficial to remember an excellent old adage—never give disease a place to start—and this can only be assured by maintaining clean aquariums and providing properly scheduled feeding practices of foods that have the necessary diet and nutritive values to keep fish in a healthy state. When fish are healthy they can easily resist many diseases, except those that are hereditary.

Living up to his name, this Siamese Fighting Fish looks as if he were about to tear into an adversary.

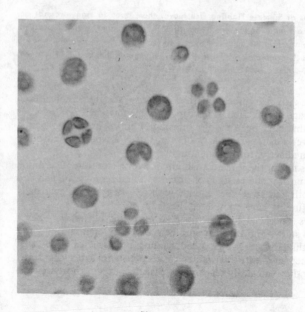

Anabantid fry are tiny and require the smallest foods as their first nourishment. Minute one-celled algae such as these are a good starting food for very young Bettas, but this must soon be replaced with foods of animal origin.

A rare brown Betta; in this color variety the fins show a greater degree of transparency than in other types. Photo by Dr. Herbert R. Axelrod.

BREEDING BETTAS

Bettas, like many other Anabantids, are bubble-nest builders. When the eggs are laid, they are picked up by the male and deposited under a nest composed of floating, sticky bubbles. While there, they are carefully tended by the male. It is not difficult to induce Bettas to spawn; the hard part is raising the fry. Fry of most Anabantids are very small and are consequently hard to feed. In addition, they are tender and require special precautions on the part of the hobbyist, especially in regard to temperature fluctuations.

Before an attempt is made to spawn Bettas, there are a number of factors that must be considered, and every effort must be made to implement as many of them as can be undertaken in a practical manner.

For success, certain points must be given careful consideration. Among these points are:

THE AQUARIUM
This should be a minimum of ten gallons in capacity. It should be thoroughly sterilized with a strong salt solution. It should have a tight-fitting full hood to prevent cold drafts from blowing across the surface of the water. This is exceedingly important, as will be detailed later.

PLANTS AND PLANTING ARRANGEMENTS
The selection of plants should be considered from the viewpoint of affording a hiding place for the female, because the courtship of Bettas is usually aggressive and, more often than not, vicious. Suitable hiding places for the female, in the form of several bunches of Cabomba (*Cabomba caroliniana*) or Ambulia (*Limnophila* species). The small fronds of these plants are also used by the male to help support the bubble-nest and prevent its breakup. The best arrangement is to plant densely in the two back corners.

SAND OR GRAVEL
It is best not to use sand or gravel in the Betta spawning tank, because it is easier for the male to see eggs which have fallen to the bottom if no such material is present. Also, absence of foreign elements in the tank further reduces chances for the presence of unwanted organisms.

WATER CONDITIONS
Extreme care should be exercised in the preparation of the water, because on this depends whether or not the attempt will be successful. The pH should be 6.8. (slightly acid) and not more than 8 degrees of hardness. It is recommended that about 50% distilled or demineralized water and ordinary tap-water should be used.

FILTRATION AND AERATION
This is necessary but should not be constant or too strong. The home waters of Siamese Fighting Fish do not have the turbulence that can be created when forceful filtration or aeration is employed. Try to arrange filtration or aeration on an intermittent basis, preferably two hours on and four hours off.

BREEDING TEMPERATURE
Although from 80° to 85° F. is a proper spawning range, the most suitable temperature is an exact 80° F. This must be maintained constantly, and this situation demands the use of a thermostatically controlled heater.

Limnophila sessiflora, Ambulia, is a good bushy plant which provides refuge for a har-assed female. Photo by Sculthorpe.

CONDITIONING BREEDING PAIR

Two weeks prior to spawning a pair of Bettas, careful selection should be made. Special attention should be paid to the size and color pattern; the female should be well rounded on the ventral side, indicating she is full of ova.

For a few days there should be a glass divider in the aquarium, and once the breeding pair have been placed, one on each side of the partition, daily observation should be made. Once the male spreads his fins, usually followed immediately by the building of the bubble-nest, the glass divider should be removed.

The male will intermittently pay attention to building the bubble-nest or chasing the female. In the actual spawning act the male will wrap himself around the female, and she will release from one to fifteen eggs. Simultaneously, the male releases his fertilizing fluid (spermatozoa) containing the sperm. As each batch of eggs is released the male catches them in his mouth and places them in the nest.

The full spawning period usually is around two to three hours, and upon completion the female should be removed. Often she is in a battered state, with badly torn fins or bitten gills plates. She should be placed into a separate small aquarium where she will have time to recuperate.

At this stage, it is advisable to feed some type of live food to the male during the period he is attending the bubble-nest. A well-fed male is not inclined to become cannibalistic.

The male embraces the female below the nest; the female is releasing the eggs.

After the eggs are released, the male leaves the female to catch them as they fall.

Once the eggs are put into the nest, the male keeps the nest under repair, also maintaining vigil on the eggs.

Now the eggs have hatched, and the youngsters will soon be able to fend for themselves.

The spawning process is a repetitive procedure; the male and female embrace under the nest many times before the female is depleted of eggs. Notice that the eggs falling here are not the first ones, for the nest already contains many eggs from previous embraces.
Photo by New York Zoological Society.

The eggs usually hatch within forty-eight hours, but the fry do not leave the nest until the yolk sac containing their initial nourishment is absorbed. This usually requires from three to four days, after which the fry become free-swimming. They will remain constantly at the surface, and any that sink are immediately picked up by the male and replaced at the surface.

During this stage of development, the young fry need plenty of food, and micro-organisms should be provided in abundance. At an age of about two weeks the fry commence to develop the air-breathing accessory organ, the labyrinth. This development requires at least five days.

It is during this period that most aquarists experience heavy losses, mainly because they fail to guard against cold drafts reaching the water surface. Every effort must be made to assure that the air immediately above the water remains at the same temperature as the water. The slightest amount of colder air passing over the surface causes the developing labyrinth to become clogged with mucus. If this happens, the fry die almost immediately.

Far too often less than 10% of a spawning is successfully brought to maturity. This can be traced to lack of special attention during the period the labyrinth is developing. Once the young fry have successfully passed this period of development, they should continue growing and reach maturity.

When the fry reach an age of between three to four months, the males should be removed to individual containers. These can be either one-gallon glass jars or, more preferably, small 2½-gallon tanks.

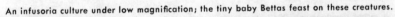

An infusoria culture under low magnification; the tiny baby Bettas feast on these creatures.

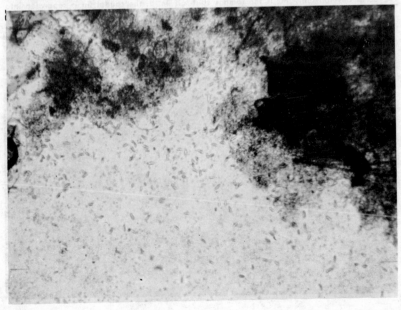

A flesh-colored female Betta. Photo by Dr. Eduard Schmidt.

A recent development, this is the famous split-tail Betta; the caudal fin is separated into two distinct lobes. Photo by Dr. Herbert R. Axelrod.

Male Bettas showing differing tail shapes; caudal of upper fish is long and tapering, whereas lower fish shows rounded development. Both photos by Dr. Herbert R. Axelrod.

FEEDING YOUNG FRY

For the first two weeks after the fry become free-swimming, there should be available quantities of infusoria. To avoid fouling the water, do not feed too much at one time. It is recommended that three tablespoonsfuls daily should be added to the water. This should be supplemented with a few drops, several times daily, of a solution containing powdered yeast. This solution is excellent for promoting continued propagation of microscopic animal life, greatly needed by the growing young fry, in the aquarium water.

When the young fry have reached an age of two weeks, newly hatched brine shrimp and finely chopped white worms may be introduced into their feeding schedule. Finely ground commercially prepared dry foods may also be offered at this time.

For sturdy growth and excellent body formation and color pattern, a daily feeding of finely scraped raw chicken liver should be given. Controlled experiments have proven that young fry fed this daily develop much faster and are more robust.

Finally, from the time the young fry are free-swimming, there should be a small feeding of extremely fine dry food. This feeding should be placed into the aquarium just before retiring for the night. Young fish require a constant supply of food. Very often, failure to realize this causes heavy losses, mainly from starvation.

These young Bettas are all of approximately the same size, a hard feat to manage with Anabantid fry. Usually, some fry grow much more quickly than their brothers and sisters, and the difference soon becomes obvious. Photo by G. J. M. Timmerman.

Commercial hatcheries all employ the decreased water depth principle in breeding Bettas and other Labyrinth fishes. Each jar arranged in rows at the rear holds a male Betta.

DECREASE OF WATER DEPTH IN THE AQUARIUM

The usual practice for breeding any of the Anabantids, and Bettas are no exception, is to fill the breeding aquarium only half way. In a ten-gallon aquarium this would amount to a depth of approximately six inches.

The reason for this is that the young fry, when first hatched, remain constantly at the surface. However, some of the weaker ones will gradually sink to the bottom. These are usually spotted by the attending male and quickly picked up in his mouth and replaced at the surface. Very often some of the young fry sink unnoticed and because of the water pressure are unable to regain the surface.

Once the fry have reached an age of one month, additional water should be added, but only in very small amounts. An excellent method is to mark one of the posts of the aquarium, on the outside, with black lines one quarter of an inch apart. Commence these markings at the surface of the water already in the aquarium.

This additional water must be exactly of the same condition as that in the aquarium. To assure this, it is advisable to prepare this additional water well ahead of the time it is to be used.

Do not pour this additional water into the aquarium. It should be added very slowly; the best method to attain this is to use a very narrow siphon, much smaller in diameter than the normal plastic air line hose. The required amount of additional water should be added not more frequently than every four days.

The vigilant male guards the nest after spawning with the female at lower right. **Straits Times** photo.

The color of the green male contrasts sharply with the color of the red Cambodia. With Bettas you can have an almost unlimited choice of coloration. Both photos by Dr. Herbert R. Axelrod.

SPAWNING PERIODS

Bettas will spawn, when in good condition, every two weeks, but this should not be permitted. Such frequent spawnings can only result in weakened fish that fail to develop to their full color and size.

Breeding pairs of Bettas should be conditioned and permitted to spawn not less than a month or six weeks between spawnings.

IMPROVEMENT THROUGH BREEDING

Many aquarists have experienced bitter disappointments, particularly from the first spawning of Bettas. Usually the young fry lack the brilliance of the parents and more often than not fail to develop to the same size.

This factor is more pronounced when two color strains are crossed. Those experiencing this situation should not be discouraged, because Bettas require at least three generations before they show their full coloration, and in many instances their normal size. Because of this factor extreme patience is required.

It took many years of dedicated hard work to bring the Betta to its present graceful beauty. Photo by New York Zoological Society.

A pair of wild-type Bettas, male to the right. Males of the original wild specimens cannot compare with the present stock in either color or finnage. Photo by G. J. M. Timmerman.

Very often in a batch of young there may be one or two that have distinct differences in color pattern, or only slight variations. These should be developed and brought to maturity, and if it so happens that there are both males and females, they should be bred. The resultant young fry from such a mating should be closely observed for any further changes in color pattern. It must be remembered that it requires many generations before a new color pattern can be bred to a true likeness of its parents. Because of this factor many aquarists, upon observing the results of their first successful spawning, become disappointed and disillusioned, thinking that their effort has not been successful. Others feel that perhaps they have commenced with inferior stock, or that it is not worth the effort because of the ultimate results.

Many of these situations would not possibly happen in nature, but when breeding is undertaken in captivity there are many factors missing, and although some may be duplicated in the home aquarium, those that are lacking may be the direct cause for the disappointment.

Actually, breeding fishes is not just a matter of placing a pair together. It is the results of the mating and the possible potential it provides which counts. There is no interest in breeding just for the sake of propagating a species. It is the development from this initial effort that provides the incentive from which is derived the interest one expects when undertaking any hobby.